Infinite Verse

Rob Clarke

© Rob Clarke, 2011
First published in 2011 by Ringo Media Group
ABN 90 108 231 090
PO Box 4, Winston Hills NSW 2153
info@infinitetalent.net

Edited by Deb Doyle (Living Proof – Book Editing)
  (deb@hotlinks.net.au)
Cover and internal text by Just Say AH! Graphic Design,
  Web Design & Print (www.justsayah.com.au)
Printed by createspace, a division of Amazon

All rights are reserved. The reserved rights under copyright
are not limited; however, no part of this publication may be
reproduced, stored in or introduced into a retrieval system,
or transmitted, in any form or by any means (electronic,
mechanical, photocopying, recording or otherwise) without
written permission from the copyright owner and publisher.

National Library of Australia Cataloguing-in-Publication
entry

Author:	Clarke, Rob, 1959–
Title:	Infinite Verse / Rob Clarke.
ISBN:	9780646564074 (pbk.)
Subjects:	Perfection – Poetry.
	Spiritual biography – Poetry.
Dewey Number:	A821.4

To your purest self

When the infinite speaks directly to a person, the words are few and absolute. The experience, as wisdom, is a pure expression of the truth.

One day, when I was out walking my dog and going through a period of heavily identifying with compulsive thinking, my world was transformed when three infinite words came into my mind: **That's not you**.

In that moment, I looked at and connected with another expression, one that was vastly different from what had been before. The sounds and images in my head continued at a moderate level, but the controlling mechanism had lost power. I realised a new talent, a new expression and the knowledge of what we're not.

Infinite Verse is about that infinite connection, and is a tool for you to transmit infinite talent through yourself and be one with yourself.

When the drama unfolds and the days grow cold
and you can't stay still or go,

When troubles come up and you buckle and fret
and a friend becomes a foe,

In that wretched daze, the infinite can arise
and new choices can unfold:

Your heavy heart is lighter, and the greyness
turns to gold.

It seems unjust that an infinite marvel
could ever be as close:

For years, you've been told to pander and please
and to passively take your dose.

But who is it who witnesses the thoughts
under the hood?

It's your purest self, a dynamic talent
that's lost or misunderstood.

The power of you is here, now, and it's good,

When you're walking or talking or eating your food.

Feel the talent rushing through your head,
heart and hip.

It's a dynamic intensity you can dare to admit.

Leaders, languages and loquaciousness abound;
old works come out anew:

Wear a beanie or a red wrist band;
be one of the special few.

Promised peace will only ever last for a day
or maybe a week.

The world turns quickly and ends with a flicker;
time perpetually plays a trick.

Realistion: what does it mean?

How can you connect with the miraculous unseen?

Look, look, and look again; appreciate and persist;

Feel the reality of you, right now:
the infinite doesn't resist.

Now you can walk in freedom, each stride anew,

Built from infinite design, the miracle you know as you;

The talent of eyes, cheeks, tongue and teeth:
a smile, a happy look;

Infinite talent is who you are, and it's always
an open book.

Sleep infinitely as the 'chat show' disappears –

Nightmares and dreams are biological affairs.

Awake when nourished by the night's subtleties;

Connect, connect, and reconnect with life's chemistry.

Look up at the galaxy with great intensity

To see the billionth star held firm in gravity.

Feel the light streaming colour through your eyes,

That awesomeness you are, before everything dies.

It's a ridiculous hour that streams and streams more,

Attached to nothing that's come before.

A dynamic power sits behind that sweet kiss,

Closer than the coolness of moist winter lips.

Do you see the cow there, chewing the cud?

Honour the moment as she stands in the mud.

Look at the meadow and the trees in the field –

That's all it takes to be whole and healed.

Please, please, connect with your purest self,

And be satisfied with life itself.

That certainty is yours and pure;

A realised heart is reassured.

Be still, breathe and let things slide,

And let this moment be your guide.

You know there's one, and only one, kind

Beyond the distractions that leave you blind.

You are an infinite display

Upon which this moment becomes day.

There's not a transformation too soon,

And it's with precision you can't assume.

No need to look with finite tone,

A character festooned with tissue and bone.

Shift your head and benefit

From a talent absolute and infinite.

When the infinite speaks directly to a person, the words are few and absolute. The experience, as wisdom, is a pure expression of the truth.

One day, when I was out walking my dog and going through a period of heavily identifying with compulsive thinking, my world was transformed when three infinite words came into my mind: **That's not you**.

In that moment, I looked at and connected with another expression, one that was vastly different from what had been before. The sounds and images in my head continued at a moderate level, but the controlling mechanism had lost power. I realised a new talent, a new expression and the knowledge of what we're not.

Infinite Verse is about that infinite connection, and is a tool for you to transmit infinite talent through yourself and be one with yourself.

To your purest self

A drowning bear is beyond his range,
a miracle lost to finite change.

To pat the paw and hold the fin –
you need not label any creature as strange.

See the eyes looking back as they sink:
it's a connection deeper than you think.

The guardians who nature trusts
infinite talent will naturally assist.

Like a hand in a tight and sticky glove,
conditioning and logic aren't above.

Connect with your eyes and face,
and replace distrust of the moment with love.

Infinite talent is in vogue and is a powerful
universal connection mode.

The infinite is the trend on this very day,
and presence is your permanent abode.

Say what you must – release the pressure
from within and without,

But before the last sound, connect with
the presence all throughout.

Let the words flow and go; jump off the fast treadmill.

Feel the wisdom in your chest; connect,
and just be still.

Sense the moisture in your eyes;
look ahead in a straight direction.

Can you see they're a sacrament
and infinite perfection?

Feel the talent power of the seer,
and connect with what is true.

Let the din and spin evaporate;
become one with the nature of you.

Finite time is maintained in thought-based,
conditioned space.

The intelligence you are evolves, and thinking
leaves no trace.

Your evidence isn't a word or story;
it's the eternal living, flowered.

This is a fearless stage at which
an inner warrior's empowered.

You might desire freedom from strife
or a break at a retreat,

But wherever you are, right here, right now,
that's the infinite seat.

Look, and see your advancement strengthen
as new insights arise.

The splendour of who you truly are
is an immaculate surprise.

Some people wait till their demise is near

To ask the question **Why am I here?**

But it's through the talent of body
that you look and hear.

Infinite pitch is in the genius of your ear.

Do you seek refuge in humble pie,
and you can't let go before you die?

Picture, **As I burn, my body will turn,
and the stream will then be dry.**

From eye and ear and mouth and lung,
there's a narrative to write,

But underneath the soul's attire,
something's not quite right.

**It's he, not she – or them, or those –
and surely can't be I.**

We begrudge, defy, and erect a fence
– could it all be a big, fat lie?

Do you tell your kin and good friends, too,
that life is not a joke?

The veils and beards and creepy figures
frighten many folk.

At any moment, a billion thoughts
disfigure humanity's face.

One by one, each thought upon one:
constriction of infinite grace.

Your interest is the infinite link, so transform
and stop 'belief'.

When the pressure drops, you see that thinking
is a whingeing little thief.

Brain and brawn; fat and water; molecules enjoined
in order –

You're never who you think you are,
and thoughts lead to disorder.

Finite tags, we give ourselves, and mindsets
to seem grand.

Being human can be a blast, but finite power's
a limited brand.

Infinite talent is all-embracing; its opposite is resistance.

You were born to realise the miracle of your existence.

The reality you are at any point in time
you truly can achieve,

Once you've had a glimpse of what makes sense
in everything you receive.

Me, myself, my mind and I: many stories
old and told,

All kept alive in your finite brain,
your talented frontal lobe.

Believe what you will and what you say,
but with just one heartfelt wish,

You'll see a talent that resides within each human,
beast and fish.

See the 'chick' with the light-blue eyes?
the dude with the thinning hair?

So many times you've dreamed the dream,
riddled with despair.

What to offer the world, my friend?
A taste of yourself, right here.

Could it all be too simplistic,
while you're tethered to custom and cheer?

Master chef, or architect,
or chair of the company board;

Activist fighter; paperback writer:
ambitions and discord.

You're all too cool when you think you rule,
but later comes the torment.

The mind is fast and cannot grasp
the impact of the present moment.

You try out many partners and you end up
feeling rotten –

Some were hot, and some were not,
and some are best forgotten.

Relationships are akin to clothes: wear them well,
and then dispose,

But please persist – you're greater than this:
it's you the infinite chose.

A billion years in your creation: this moment
is your demonstration.

The smallest events are all immense
in this moment's jubilation.

To proceed, go direct, and with intent,
you surely will detect

An aliveness in you so different
it becomes self-evident.

When you've thought it all through
and your cash is all spent,

Connect again and again and again
with infinite talent.

Your finite thoughts are just ideas you use
to earn your bread,

But before all the drama and turmoil inside,
the infinite was there, unsaid.

See the bend in the river and the rain come together

As your heart and consciousness blend forever.

Awaken to feel the infinite stream;
you have been blessed so much.

It's a moment you cannot rush
— that first time, the infinite touch.

A finite imprint is amassed
with each and every thought.

Constant brain discharge is spent on memory
and battles hard fought.

The finite mind that dominates is a game
that can't be won.

You're more than you can ever dream up,
and of you there's only one.

Soldier and dog; sailor and seal:
what suffering has there been?

'An eye for an eye!' till you see those eyes
return the look, serene.

'Water under the bridge'; laughter; hope;
the pain we see on TV –

Nothing's over till you're finished with finite time
and history.

Rich people plan to increase the costs
because that's what got them there –

Ask any entrepreneur who's charming and disarming:
money's difficult to share.

'Hollywood hunks' and 'champagne tarts' have a talent
they've failed to see.

They make good drama for 'slackers' in pyjamas,
but will they set you free?

The intelligence behind a grain of sand
came before the finite mind.

An apple; some lettuce; some salt on the tongue
– eat simply; be humble and kind.

Sense the pressure of your teeth on your food,
and listen as they grind.

The fruit of the vine and the flesh of the swine
are objects of the linear mind.

A country's bones lie under monarch stones,
and rebels are without a clue.

The blood and the tears came only last year:
realisation must be due.

All seems well when you're in the groove,
but soon it's a different scene.

Life loses its lustre; you must come clean
and let the infinite intervene.

To care is 'one,' to dote is 'two', and you've cried
for 'three' and 'four'.

Remember when you last shook the hand
of a friend who is no more?

Do you want for a son or a sister who's fun
or just do your bit and learn some?

The precision that's you is the ultimate state
and a moment always welcome.

A child is born and crawls and walks;
then it's school bags, e-books and peers.

We climb a tree; get stung by a bee;
fall over and hurt our rears.

The passing years bring laughs and tears
and problems when we're still young,

But when we're older, we pay for the past
and wonder why life's no fun.

Sympathy for the surfer; rhapsody for the worker;

Shift your attention, city banker:
the door is closing further.

History is fine and science fair;
feel the truth of this moment laid bare.

Separate the dots and see what's not;
look up from your high, high chair.

Arise from bed: there's the talking head;
you're once again being misled.

You read the paper – it's all too much,
so you sit and stare instead.

Listen to a new voice and hear it say,
Life can be an awesome ride.

Practise what you know is true;
stop, look and listen, and let all thoughts slide.

Some say the world will end today;
their neuroses and neurons lie in wait.

There are symbols, myths and legends aplenty,
but you don't take the bait.

You're precisely the infinite that is you,
so who needs navel gazing?

Awakening starts with connection,
feels good and becomes amazing.

You are present here and now;
in this moment you're substantiated.

Infinite talent is who you are;
from that marvel, all life originated.

You've neither been nor come before,
but do these thoughts make you blue?

Alone – or all one?
Could it be just a point of view?

Whether your eyes are open or closed
or your fingers feel the touch,

All you need is an interest;
then quickly you will trust

The infinite joy you already are,
and your body will agree.

To connect or not to connect right now?
This moment is always free.

When infinite talent uploads,
a synchronised life explodes.

The body reacts with satisfying impact;
it's the end of highs and lows.

Wetlands, salt pans and shifting sands
are all talents far beyond prose.

Spend time in nature and come ever closer
to the miracle that ebbs and flows.

From me to you, 'cause I was born in a thought zoo
in the West:

Don't ever settle for anything less
than absolute fullness expressed.

You're no one's shadow; you're infinite talent,
even when asleep.

Make the connection: you are this day;
moment upon moment is yours to keep.

Atoms in motion trigger commotion;
you could say it's a quantum potion –

Creative potential; incredible intention;
a celestial devotion;

An intelligence so wondrous
it induces the infinite romantic –

A cosmic **joie de vivre** for all,
the nemesis of pedantic.

Don't liquidate this moment;
just let the infinite arise.

The complaining mind has no hold on you,
and this you'll realise.

The audio-visuals in your head
decrease as the pressure comes down.

You are supreme; you're not a dream;
feel the talent of your crown.

A new renaissance is afoot,
and new, conscious leaders value it.

Hell's shutting up shop, so take a cue:
infinite talent won't quit.

Connect with your purest self-expression;
feel radiance and trust.

When you bring new talent into the world,
connect infinitely as you thrust.

Religion means 'a reconnection',
so what in the world do we expect

If we choose not to connect? What's left?
A person suffering disconnect.

The blossom, the perfume and the bee
existed before the faith.

Their intimacy's carried on the wind,
the air in which we bathe.

Have a hot drink and a piece of toast;
talk for hours without end.

Spit the dummy now and then;
survive by learning to pretend.

The game of life is so fast paced,
the product of a finite mind.

What expression are you within:
the restless or the still kind?

To believe or disbelieve?
Thought systems: what do they mean?

It's so obvious, when you've seen it,
that spirit's in every gene.

It's now; it's instant, an elusive caress;
the sparkle and the shine.

To dance now and to be divine:
to pass on the infinite bloodline.

Tick! Tock! The mind doesn't stop
– the finite stream of fakes.

Thinking is a talent, and has its place,
but have you ever had any breaks?

To seek awakening by compulsively thinking
is something we do in haste,

But there's much at stake, and the infinite moment
is the beauty you must taste.

When you cannot sleep and thought is there
to always steal your peace,

And in the dark, the mind repeats the streaming
that won't cease,

Connect with your purest self,
with your hands, legs, face and chest.

Don't be anxious about anything else:
be at one, in infinite rest.

In this moment, be seduced
and let finite thinking be reduced.

Through you, the infinite flow of life
is beautifully produced.

When you have nothing on your mind
and simplicity persists,

You'll thrill to a silent passion
as each molecule quivers and twists.

Does knowledge imbue perception,
and what colours your sense of reason?

Love, wisdom, joy and connection are yours,
whatever the current season.

The infinite holds the smallest thumb
and the petal on the smallest flower.

You are the now, the one and the all,
the attraction that creates this hour.

Who or what are we,
without thought after thought?

And what remains
when the talk shows halt?

Could there be an experience,
a wonderful affair –

The exactness of your purest self,
unattached to skin and hair?

With intent, take one look
at the stars and the moon:

They're a perfect encounter
between you and that infinite room.

With presence, we dissolve the dream
of what went before,

When we were totally led by the finite –
but it can't torment us any more.

The ego thinks that it's the life,
and then it leads to many types:

The strict believer; the extreme-thrill seeker;
the one who wears the stripes;

The lucky guy; the 'hard done by';
the dangerous; the shy;

The cruel kind; the loud and proud:
through aggressiveness, some will die.

The finite stream of the thinking mind
is very rarely rewarding;

It's a sideline to awakening,
through which we keep ourselves from transcending.

Caught up in all the silliness and unrest;
trying to survive at our best –

Coexistence isn't that easy
when daily life's an ongoing test.

The moon's **always** full,
and the sun's **always** high;

There's no conflict
between those two powers in the sky.

Hear the wisdom that resides
in the philosopher, sage and mystic:

In the new renaissance,
the infinite is expressed in verse and music.

A finite thought can be
of a sad or beautiful world view;

You can make a big statement
from something that's not really new.

You can become troubled
without ever breaking a finite law –

Do you always believe in everything
you think you heard or saw?

To give and to take:
do they cause the dramas to rebound?

Right here, right now,
what causes the earth to be round?

There's a silent intelligence
that very rarely counts –

Feel your facial expression now,
before the pressure mounts.

Fancy stories are told
in dining bars and prison yards;

Blue collar; white collar;
the keeper's never far.

Knuckle down and get on with it,
and keep your thoughts within –

No one can hear what you're saying
as you stand and scratch your chin.

You might or might not have participated
in extraordinary things;

Fear's a hindrance to creativity,
but not for all human beings.

A transformation's begun,
and your bio-network knows what to do;

Now, you don't always 'mind the mind' that thinks,
This is false, and **That is true.**

Your journey, if you choose it,
is to connect with your purest self –

Let infinite talent stream ... and stream ...
through every living cell.

You've found that place of perfect rest
and entered through that door,

So surf that most divine of moments:
the joy and thrill you're engineered for.

Infinite Talent

By infinite design, you exist – at this moment.
Infinite talent is here right now,
so why not choose to connect right now?

You're not who you think you are;
you're infinite talent,
even before a thought 'tells you so'
– that's how powerful you are.

To buy online:
www.infinitetalent.net

www.ingramcontent.com/pod-product-compliance
Lightning Source LLC
Chambersburg PA
CBHW040732240426
43666CB00043B/11